DISASTER!

Disaster can come to anyone, anywhere. It can come to a Roman writer, watching a great mountain throw fire and ash into the sky, or to a fireman in the Ukraine, hurrying to an emergency in a nuclear reactor. It can come in a deadly cloud to a young man sleeping in Bhopal, or slowly take away life from a mother of six in Uganda.

Disaster can be on the other side of the world – and yet from the safety of our own homes we can watch it happen, minute by minute. It can bring death and misery to the poorest village or the richest city, from Banda Aceh to New Orleans.

And disaster brings extraordinary stories of lucky escapes, terrible mistakes, and great bravery. Here you will read about human beings at their very best – inventive, caring, thoughtful, and strong – and at their worst . . .

OXFORD BOOKWORMS LIBRARY

Factfiles

Disaster!

Stage 4 (1400 headwords)

Factfiles Series Editor: Christine Lindop

MARY McINTOSH

Disaster!

OXFORD UNIVERSITY PRESS

OXFORD
UNIVERSITY PRESS

Great Clarendon Street, Oxford, OX2 6DP, United Kingdom

Oxford University Press is a department of the University of Oxford.
It furthers the University's objective of excellence in research, scholarship,
and education by publishing worldwide. Oxford is a registered trade
mark of Oxford University Press in the UK and in certain other countries

ISBN: 978 0 19 423395 8   Book
ISBN: 978 0 19 463804 3   Book and audio pack

Printed in Great Britain by Ashford Colour Press Ltd.

Word count (main text): 14,791

For more information on the Oxford Bookworms Library,
visit www.oup.com/elt/gradedreaders

ACKNOWLEDGEMENTS

Alamy Stock Photo pp.12 (earthquake safety drill/epa european pressphoto agency b.v.),
63 (Eyam village/PearlBucknall), 65 (Eyam graves/Geoffrey Morgan), 68 (AIDS orphan/
imageBROKER), 72 (draught land/Tom Wang); Bridgeman Art Library Ltd p.6 (Pompeii (fresco),
Roman, (1st century AD)/Museo Archeologico Nazionale, Naples, Italy); Getty Images pp.viii
(relief workers/TARIK TINAZAY), 4 (Pompeii, Italy/O. Louis Mazzatenta), 7 (collapsed building/
Dario Mitidieri), 9 (Tangshan earthquake aftermath/Sovfoto), 10 (earthquake-torn Tangshan/
Bettmann), 13 (Great Hanshin Earthquake/The Asahi Shimbun), 17 (monk by shipwreck/
Romeo Gacad/AFP), 18 (humanitarian aid/Dimas Ardian), 21 (Hurricanes Katrina/ROBYN
BECK), 23 (New Orleans flood/POOL), 24 (Katrina victims/David Portnoy), 27 (Great fire of
London/Time Life Pictures), 29 (Illustration of George Fox/Bettmann), 31 (Titanic postcard/
Time Life Pictures), 32 (Titanic living room/Roger Viollet), 34 (Titanic survivors/Krista Few),
36 (Titanic shipwreck/Ralph White), 38 (deadly gas leak, India/Bettmann), 40 (Bhopal Gas
Tragedy/Mint), 42 (Space Shuttle Challenger crew/Corbis), 44 (Space Shuttle explosion/
Bettmann), 46 (Columbia Disaster/Handout), 49 (Exxon Valdez/Natalie B. Fobes), 51 (Exxon
Valdez oil spill/Anchorage Daily News), 55 (Chernobyl/East News), 59 (Chernobyl/Sean Gallup),
60 (abandoned funfair Prypyat/Sergei Supinsky/AFP), 61 (Chernobyl protest/Sergei Supinsky),
70 (world AIDS Day/RAVEENDRAN), cover (firefighters/Bill Stormont).

Cover: Bill Stormont/Corbis

CONTENTS

Can we survive?

Dr Stephen Hawking, one of the most famous scientists of our time, recently asked, 'How can the human race survive the next 100 years?' In two days, 16,000 people had contacted him and offered him their answers.

Behind Stephen Hawking's question is the idea that our way of life is leading us towards disaster – a disaster so big that people will no longer be able to live on the Earth 100 years from now.

So what disasters is Stephen Hawking expecting? What is wrong with the way we live? It seems that he is worried about how we use energy, and how we look after the Earth's environment. We shall consider some of these questions in more detail in this book.

Some natural disasters (like volcanoes and earthquakes) are beyond human control, because the causes lie deep inside the Earth. Natural disasters usually happen very suddenly, and they often cause much pain and suffering to the people living nearby. But there are other disasters for which human beings are responsible. A good example is the *Titanic* disaster, when that great ship sank to the bottom of the dark waters of the Atlantic Ocean.

In this book you will read about many types of disasters. No one can offer all the answers to questions about why disasters happen – not even extremely clever people like Stephen Hawking. However, we can consider ways of preventing disasters, and ways of helping people to manage the big changes that disasters bring to their lives.

1 Natural disasters

It has been said that there are no truly natural disasters – all disasters are actually caused by human beings. This is an extreme opinion, and most people would immediately disagree. But perhaps we can take a little bit of truth from those words.

The fact is that the poorest people suffer most when disaster hits. This is probably because they cannot choose where to live, their homes are not made of strong materials, and they are not well informed. Their lives are therefore more open to danger.

Many of the people who lost their lives and their homes in the Asian tsunami (see chapter 1.3) and in Hurricane Katrina (see chapter 1.4) were poor, and they were completely unprepared. But governments too were badly organized and poorly prepared for this kind of emergency. So while the causes of those disasters, and many others, were natural, many of the effects were made worse by human weakness.

1.1   Vesuvius

In the twenty-first century 1 million people live and work in the crowded, noisy city of Naples, in Italy. From one day to the next, many of them probably do not lift their eyes to look up at Vesuvius, the great volcano which rises nearly 1,300 metres high to the east of the city.

In the year AD 79, nearly 2,000 years earlier, the people of the busy town of Pompeii were hurrying about their lives. Pompeii is 20 kilometres south-east of Naples, and it is only 10 kilometres from the great volcano. At that time, Pompeii was a rich town of 20,000 people with a busy port and market. All around the town were the beautiful homes of rich men and their families.

Then, on 24 August, everything changed forever. In the middle of the morning, the ground began to shake. Cups fell off tables, and holes appeared in the ground. People remembered the disastrous earthquake that had hit Pompeii in AD 62. Was this the beginning of another earthquake?

Dogs started to bark loudly, birds flew away, and then a strange silence seemed to fall over the town. At midday, a great cloud of grey ash rose up from Vesuvius and into the air. That afternoon, with a terrible noise a thousand times louder than thunder, the top of the volcano was blown 20 kilometres into the air, and sheets of flame lit up the darkened sky. Vesuvius was erupting!

A south-east wind quickly blew the cloud of ash towards the town of Pompeii. People panicked and tried to escape. But for many, it was too late. In two days, the town was covered

Pompeii and Mount Vesuvius

in 4 metres of ash and stones. About 2,000 people were killed by the cloud of hot gases and ash. Others were buried in a mountain of hot, wet mud which caused immediate death.

The small town of Herculaneum, which lies between Vesuvius and the sea, met a more violent end than Pompeii. After the first eruption of Vesuvius, many people had left Herculaneum. Those who remained thought that they would be safe, because the wind was not blowing the ash and smoke towards them.

However, that was a false hope. One day after the first eruption, Herculaneum was suddenly covered by a river of hot ash and mud. In a few hours, the town was buried under 20 metres of hardened rock from the volcano.

In some ways, this eruption of Vesuvius was just like any other disaster caused by volcanoes. People died miserable deaths, and the families and survivors had to learn to make new lives for themselves. So why do we remember this eruption of Vesuvius as something special? Let us consider how we have come to know about life in Italy at that time.

In AD 79, Pompeii and Herculaneum were controlled by the great city of Rome. We know much about Rome and its people through books written in the Latin language. Virgil and Pliny were famous writers of that time. In fact, there were two writers named Pliny, and both of them were caught in the eruption. Pliny the Younger survived and wrote a detailed diary about the disaster, but his uncle, Pliny the Elder, was killed.

However, we have more than just books to tell us about the world of the Romans at that time.

The eruption of Vesuvius killed people suddenly, in the middle of a very normal day. Then the mud covered their bodies, which stayed untouched for many centuries. This had

A wall painting in Pompeii

a surprising result: today, Pompeii and Herculaneum show us how life was in these two Roman towns in the first century AD.

By digging down through the mud, people have discovered the houses and streets of the two towns, with their shops, street signs, and paintings. They have also found the theatres, the bars, the kitchens, and the town baths. From these places, and from the things found there, many interesting facts have been discovered about life in Roman times. For example, in the open-air theatre of Pompeii the bones of dead gladiators have been discovered. Gladiators fought animals and each other – and often died – while crowds of people watched and enjoyed themselves.

In the two towns today you can see the plates, cups, coins, rings, and bracelets that people used and wore on that day long ago. There is also graffiti – writing on the walls – which tells us what people were feeling and thinking, just as graffiti does today. Perhaps the people of Roman times were really quite similar to us today!

So the disaster which hit the people of Pompeii and Herculaneum in AD 79 has given us a very real and meaningful lesson in the history of Italy and the Roman people.

1.2   Earthquakes

In London, many tourists like to visit a special 'earthquake machine'. This allows you to stand in a room which looks like a supermarket, to see the room shaking, to hear the shelves trembling, and to feel the floor moving up and down. It is almost like experiencing a real earthquake.

A tourist may feel excited when the ground moves and tins fall off shelves. But an earthquake machine cannot match the horror of a real earthquake – the horror of seeing your normal world disappear, and the pain of seeing your family die before your eyes. Yet that is what has happened to thousands of earthquake victims through the centuries until the present day.

After an earthquake, Kobe, Japan, 1995

In chapter 1.3 you can read about the earthquake that caused the 2004 tsunami, when water flooded many countries near the Indian Ocean. But we begin with the worst earthquake disaster of the twentieth century, which hit the city of Tangshan, north-east China, in 1976. That is followed by the story of Japan's Kobe earthquake in 1995.

Tangshan, 1976

China has a long history of earthquakes. In fact, the first machine to measure earthquakes was made by a Chinese scientist in the second century AD. In modern times, scientists use the Richter scale, which gives earthquakes a number from 0 to 10. Every day in the world there are about 1,000 small earthquakes at level 2 that people do not notice; at the other end of the scale, the strongest earthquake in the history of the world, which happened in Chile in 1960, measured 9.5 on the Richter scale.

Tangshan is about 200 kilometres east of Beijing, the capital city of China. For several weeks in the summer of 1976, strange signs had been reported in and around this busy city of 1.5 million people. In some deep wells around Tangshan, water levels seemed to rise and fall several times, and other wells began to smell of gas.

During the first weeks of July that year, animals started behaving strangely too. One family noticed that their chickens ran around wildly and refused to eat. A father reported that his family's goldfish jumped out of its bowl! When the children put the fish back in its bowl, it jumped out again! (Perhaps animals have special ways of knowing about danger.) Towards the end of July, even more strange things began to happen. People reported that the sky was full of lights brighter than lightning, and noises louder than thunder.

Tangshan, 1976

However, none of these signs had prepared the people of Tangshan for the disaster that actually hit them in the early hours of the morning of 28 July 1976.

The earthquake started 11 kilometres under the city and measured 8.2 on the Richter scale. It lasted only 15 seconds, but those 15 seconds were enough to kill thousands of people who were sleeping peacefully in their beds. Just a few hours later, there was another earthquake. This one measured 7.1 on the Richter scale – smaller than the first, but very deadly. It hit the city as the survivors were beginning to pull themselves from under the rocks and stones that used to be their homes. Many rescuers who were trying to help the first victims became victims of the second earthquake.

In those short moments, the city of Tangshan was completely destroyed. The earthquake was 400 times more powerful than the nuclear bomb that hit the Japanese city of Hiroshima in World War Two. People even died 200 kilometres away, in Beijing.

The Tangshan earthquake was the worst earthquake disaster of the twentieth century. The Chinese government reported that a quarter of a million people died, but other reports suggest that the true number of victims was nearer to half a million. The truth is difficult to know. In that ghost city with no fresh water, no electricity, and no food, there was great danger of disease from the thousands of dead bodies. So there was no time to find the names or count the true numbers of all the victims before the bodies were buried. This has caused much sadness to many families, who would normally remember their loved ones at the Chinese festival of Qing Ming.

In the middle of so much sadness we can, however, report two stories with happy endings. One is from Qinglong, which

Tangshan was completely destroyed

is 115 kilometres from Tangshan. Government workers who had received scientific warnings of a possible earthquake organized tents for 200,000 people, and that is where they slept on the night of the disaster. Although 180,000 buildings were destroyed in Qinglong, not a single person died because of the earthquake.

The other story comes from a man called Ming Jiahua. When the earthquake hit, he and his friends were working deep under the ground. Frightened for their lives, they came up for air as quickly as possible. There were 15,000 people working underground on that terrible night, but only thirteen men died. That was truly wonderful – and lucky!

Kobe, 1995
Like China, Japan has always had earthquakes. To give Japanese people a better chance of surviving these disasters, they have special training in school, and new homes in Japan must keep people safe during earthquakes. Some Japanese children also enjoy earthquake computer games, which give them the feeling of what a real earthquake is like!

On 1 September 1923 there was a very big earthquake in Tokyo, which killed 143,000 people. Japanese people still remember 1 September as National Disaster Prevention Day. However, neither thoughts about that disaster nor all the earthquake preparations were enough to help the people of Kobe when an earthquake hit their city in southern Japan.

At 5.45 a.m. on Tuesday 17 January 1995, when many people were still asleep, the ground began to shake. Roofs fell in, roads suddenly disappeared, and cars and houses were destroyed. An earthquake measuring 7.2 on the Richter scale had hit the city of Kobe.

The destruction was unbelievable. One train station fell into pieces, destroying many cars in its car park. A huge road

Japanese schoolchildren preparing for an earthquake exercise

simply fell down to one side. The lines of the high-speed 'bullet train' broke in eight places.

One fifth of the city's population – about 310,000 people – were left homeless, 6,440 buildings were destroyed, and 6,000 people were killed.

There were many problems for the survivors and the rescuers. Many parts of the city had no water, either for drinking or for washing. Many roads were destroyed, so it was impossible at first to take food, water, and medicine to injured people. And the weather was cold!

Although people were freezing with cold in some places, there were unwanted fires in other places. In fact, fire spread through many parts of the city, and destroyed as much as the actual earthquake.

There were many sad stories of death and loneliness. People heard the voice of a little girl who was trapped under a house. '*Okaasan, okaasan* (Mother, mother),' she called. But the calling stopped at seven o'clock in the evening: the rescuers did not arrive in time.

About one hour after the earthquake, one man was standing at a bus stop, waiting for a bus to go to work. Perhaps he was hoping that if he did a normal day's work, then life would return to normal. But the bus never arrived.

In the late twentieth century, the Japanese people had started to believe that scientists could always warn them when an earthquake was going to hit Japan. People also felt that, after the experience of so many earthquakes, they were better prepared for disaster. In fact, it seems that scientists can never fully protect people from earthquakes and their destruction. No one can control nature.

Kobe 1995:
Fire destroyed as much
as the earthquake

1.3 The Asian Tsunami

Until recently, only the Japanese (and scientists who study natural disasters) knew that a tsunami is a huge wave caused by an earthquake under the sea. Then, on 26 December 2004, the word 'tsunami' entered the English language.

The Asian tsunami was caused by an earthquake measuring 9.3 on the Richter scale – the second largest ever known in the history of the Earth. It started 30 kilometres under the Indian Ocean and 160 kilometres west of Sumatra, one of the islands of Indonesia. Just before 8 o'clock on the morning of 26 December, the earthquake sent waves through the Indian Ocean. At first those waves were not very big, so no warning was given that they would develop into a tsunami. In fact, there was a delay of several hours before the waves hit the coast. In many places, the waves were 20 metres high and they travelled at speeds of 800 kilometres per hour.

Can you imagine a wall of water higher than a house, moving faster than an aeroplane, destroying everything in its path – trees, cars, houses, and people? Can you imagine how it feels when that wall of water hits you and pushes you under?

Well, that is what happened to many people on the coasts of Indonesia, Thailand, Sri Lanka, and India. The tsunami even hit the east coast of Africa, as far away as Somalia and South Africa. Not surprisingly, hundreds of thousands of people lost their lives, and more than a million lost their homes. The Asian tsunami was the worst tsunami in history.

Countries hit by the Asian Tsunami

Bangladesh

Myanmar
(Burma)

Thailand

Malaysia

Indonesia

Sumatra

Banda Aceh

India

Sri
Lanka

Indian Ocean

Somalia

Madagascar

Kenya

Tanzania

South
Africa

There are many stories about what happened during and after the tsunami. Before the disaster, a young man named Erwin sold flowers in the market at Banda Aceh, in Indonesia. When the tsunami hit, he was riding home on his motorbike. Like many others, he found a high place which offered him safety – a small bridge over a fast-flowing river. The water under the bridge was black with mud, and it was full of broken cars and dead bodies.

At that moment, everyone on the bridge was simply glad to be alive. But suddenly they heard a cry, 'Papa, papa!' There was a little girl in the middle of the river, holding onto a piece of wood.

Most people were too frightened to go near the water, but Erwin decided that he could not let a little girl disappear down a river of death. So he stepped into the fast-moving water and tried to make his way towards her. After fifteen minutes he finally reached her, but he couldn't lift her because her foot was trapped and she was in great pain.

In the end, another man, Heru Kurniwan, came to help Erwin. He held the child's hand, while Erwin kept their heads above the water. The little girl was saved, but Erwin returned to his own private disaster. He discovered that his five-year-old son had died in the tsunami. We do not know what happened to Heru.

And that is the story of so many people during the days that followed the disaster. The waters of the tsunami separated people from one another, and many still do not know what happened to their loved ones. Were they alive or dead? Were they injured? Were their bodies somewhere on land or somewhere at sea? For the survivors, this uncertainty is very cruel.

Many countries offered help after the tsunami. Some sent

After the tsunami, Thailand 2004

Many countries sent food and medicines

food and medicines, and some helped to rebuild homes, schools, and hospitals. Others helped to organize lists of lost people, so that people could make contact with the rest of their family – if that was at all possible. Here is another story from Banda Aceh in Indonesia.

Muhammad Ali had said goodbye to his daughter Sri Handayani a few weeks before the tsunami as she left on a family visit. When the tsunami hit their home, Muhammad Ali had no idea where his daughter was. For six long months he heard nothing, and he thought that she must be dead. Then he saw a list of people who were looking for their families. The desperate father read the list, hoping that he would see his daughter's name. It was there! Sri Handayani was alive! Once they knew the good news, the whole family was impatient to be together again. 'I thought you were dead!' cried Sri Handayani. 'I thought *you* were dead!' said Muhammad Ali.

Sri Handayani has now decided that she wants to be a policewoman, so that she can help other people.

After the tsunami, there were many stories of bravery in the face of disaster. One of them is about five women, Neneh, Cut, Nur, Nuraida, and Suastri, who lost parents and grandchildren, brothers and sisters, husbands and friends on that terrible day. After the tsunami, they lived for nearly two months in tents. They knew that they had lost their homes, but they still dreamed of being back in their village. They had lost everything except hope.

When the five women returned to their village, there was no electricity and no clean water. But rescue workers from other countries realized that these women were strong and hard-working. They gave them tents to live in, and helped them to get electricity and water. In the end, the women were able to earn money by helping to clean up the village. With that money, they could begin their lives again, start small businesses, and help the village to rise from the dead.

In the middle of disaster, we sometimes hear surprising stories. The tsunami hit many poor people, but it also hit a large number of tourists. Tilly Smith, aged ten, had been learning about tsunamis in her geography lessons at school in England, before she went to Thailand on holiday with her family. When she saw that the sea was moving quickly back from the beach she immediately recognized the signs of danger. She warned her family and other tourists, and they all left the beach and went to higher land – just in time.

One year later, Tilly and her family went back to Thailand to a special celebration remembering the tsunami. Tilly spoke to thousands of people, and her message was simple. It was not death that won that day – it was people, and their kindness, bravery, and love.

1.4 Hurricane Katrina

Imagine sitting at home, looking out of your window, and seeing distant ships moving along a river above your head.

That may seem strange, but that is what people may really see any day in the city of New Orleans, in the southern USA. This is because people in New Orleans live about 2 metres below sea level. Their city has water on three sides. To the east lies Lake Borgne, to the north lies Lake Pontchartrain, and to the south lies the Mississippi River. The city is also only 100 kilometres north of the Gulf of Mexico, where violent storms and hurricane winds are part of normal life.

Over more than 200 years, the people of New Orleans have developed a system of walls (called levees) which control the water that flows in and around their city. The 560 kilometres of levees help to protect the city from floods, but they often need to be repaired.

In recent years there have been many violent storms in the Gulf of Mexico, and city planners have been discussing the need to make the system better for a long time. Nothing had actually

happened, however, when Hurricane Katrina suddenly arrived in August 2005.

Hurricane Katrina started over the sea in the Gulf of Mexico on 23 August. A few days later it hit the coast of the southern USA with winds of 240 kilometres per hour. Many towns and cities suffered from the effects of the hurricane, but no city was more badly hit than New Orleans.

Two bridges and three of the levees which protect that great city were damaged by Hurricane Katrina. Suddenly water was flooding into homes and offices, churches and prisons, and nearly 80 per cent of the city was under water. Michael Homan, a university teacher, reports that he swam to his office at Xavier University, and then he swam home again. He was desperately hoping that the water around his house would go down – but he was disappointed.

New Orleans, August 2005

The immediate effect of so much water was that there was no electricity, very little drinking water, and very little food. Most roads were unusable, and most phones did not work. Hospital patients had no food, and some died as a result. Old people drowned in their homes. The situation became worse as toilets stopped working, and dead bodies began to appear in the flood waters.

Family and friends, the police, the army – many, many people offered help. Helicopters picked people up from the roofs of their houses, neighbours filled boats with food to give to friends in need, and music-lovers offered to organize music festivals to make money for the victims.

But the disaster also brought out the worst in some people. Criminals broke shop windows and stole everything. Some walked through the city showing everyone their stolen jewellery, watches, and clothes.

Some of the worst stories came from the prisons of New Orleans as the flood waters rose. Dan Bright was in prison when the hurricane hit, and he tells us that the prison guards simply disappeared. 'There were only the prisoners, the water was up to our chest, and there were no lights. So we found pipes, and we broke windows and climbed out.

'Then, when we got out, it was night-time, and the city was completely dark. The police just put us on boats, brought us

A helicopter rescuing flood victims

to a bridge, and left us there for three days without food or water. They just left us there. They (the police) had water, but they weren't giving us any. We couldn't stand up. They made us sit down. We couldn't even go to the toilet.'

Another terrible place was the New Orleans Superdome. Normally people go to this huge building to watch games of American football, but after Hurricane Katrina 25,000 people lived there for days and weeks in unhealthy conditions, without food, water, or toilets. The smell there was so bad that doctors covered their faces as they walked about. In the end, the people in the Superdome were moved to other cities, but not before many people had died or fallen ill.

Every death caused by a disaster is sad, but in fact 'only'

Waiting for help outside the Superdome

1,836 people lost their lives during Hurricane Katrina. Perhaps more important than the number of deaths was the fact that nearly 500,000 people lost their homes, and it cost 81.2 billion US dollars to repair the damage. Katrina was by far the most expensive natural disaster in US history.

It is easy to be clever after a disaster and to say, 'Why didn't they do this, why didn't they do that?' But what lessons can we learn from the experience of a disaster like Hurricane Katrina, in one of the richest countries of the world?

Firstly, it seems that there was a need for better plans to move people away from the disaster: stronger and better roads and railways. Secondly, it is clear that the earth walls in New Orleans – the levees – needed to be repaired more carefully and more often. Many people have asked whether New Orleans should be rebuilt in a different, safer, place far away from the floods – but would that new city still be New Orleans? One thing is certain: making a 'new' New Orleans, or rebuilding the old one as a safe, clean city, is going to take a very long time.

2   Human error

Days, weeks, months, or years after a disaster, it is often easy to look back and see where things went wrong. This is perhaps even more true of disasters that are caused by human error – usually small mistakes with very big results.

The Great Fire of London in 1666 started as a small kitchen fire, but its effects changed London for ever. The *Titanic* and the *Exxon Valdez* disasters happened at sea. Both were caused by an unbelievable confidence that nothing could go wrong, and that confidence resulted in serious mistakes which are still discussed today. The Bhopal and Chernobyl disasters resulted from scientific experiments that went badly wrong. These disasters raise questions about management and science. Is it possible for governments to pass laws to make science safe? That seems doubtful. In the end, every person, every worker, has to have their own understanding of the law. And people make mistakes.

The *Challenger* and *Columbia* space shuttle disasters are extreme examples of human error. On the one hand, the USA was spending hundreds of millions of dollars on its space programme, and the government and the scientists felt a great need to succeed. On the other hand, it is very clear that all the scientists, including the crew, were very worried the night before *Challenger* began its flight. So why was *Challenger* allowed to fly? Perhaps the scientists were too sensitive to the opinions of the government, the newspapers, and the TV reporters. Science is wonderful, but people are only human.

2.1 The Great Fire of London

In the seventeenth century, London was a city full of rats: rats in the streets, rats in the houses, rats in the shops. In the year 1665, thousands of people in London died from a terrible disease carried by rats. Nobody felt safe from disease and death.

The next year, 1666, there was a long hot summer. People were glad to enjoy the sunshine, and they felt that it probably helped the city to get rid of disease. But in fact the disease was finally destroyed by something much more powerful: fire.

It was two o'clock in the morning on Monday 2 September 1666. Thomas Farynor, who made bread for King Charles the Second, was asleep above his shop, near the River Thames and London Bridge. It was time for his men to start preparing bread for the king's breakfast; the king liked fresh bread in the morning.

One of Mr Farynor's men woke up and went to light the kitchen fires. Mr Farynor kept a lot of wood in his kitchen, ready to cook the bread every day. That morning, the man discovered that some wood had caught fire, and the kitchen was beginning to burn!

Quickly, the man woke Mr Farynor and shouted 'Fire! Fire!' Soon the whole house was awake, and people were running everywhere, trying to escape. Mr Farynor escaped by climbing on to the roof of the next house. One woman was not so lucky. She stayed in the house, perhaps hoping to save some of her money, but she burned to death.

In a short time the fire spread to other houses, and a strong wind blew the flames towards the west. More and more people panicked, and they all tried to save their valuables. The fire moved quickly through the old city. The houses were made of wood, and were built very close together in narrow streets. As the fire spread, it destroyed everything in its way, but it could not cross the River Thames. After some time, it reached the buildings beside the river where rich businessmen kept strange and exciting things from across the seas. Then London began to smell of hot pepper, and burning brandy began to flow like a river through the streets!

We have some very good descriptions of the fire that night. Samuel Pepys was an important man in the government of King Charles, and every day he wrote a diary about his life in London at that time. He wrote that one of the women in his house 'called us up about three in the morning, to tell us of a great fire in the city. So I rose . . . and went to her window

People trying to escape with their valuables

. . . I thought it far enough off, and so went to bed again to sleep.'

By the time Pepys woke up again, the fire had already burnt three hundred houses in London. He went to King Charles to tell him that the fire was really serious.

As Lord Mayor of London, Sir Thomas Bludworth was one of the most important and powerful men in the city. He thought that the fire could be put out easily, so he tried to organize the fire-fighting. But he soon realized that the job was more difficult than he expected, and left the city in a panic. It was then that King Charles and his brother James decided to try and help.

The king soon realized that the fire was completely out of control. He called a meeting of the Privy Council – a group of important men who could help and advise him. Together they decided to make several 'fire posts' in the city, where the fire-fighters were given everything they needed to fight the fire. King Charles led the fight, and he gave a special guinea coin to every helper. (One guinea was worth a bit more than one English pound, which was a lot of money in those days.) He worked for thirty hours without sleep, and he was much loved for his bravery.

King Charles and his men decided to clear part of the city by pulling down some houses, so that the fire had nothing to burn there. This stopped the fire, and by Wednesday 5 September 1666, the fire was finally under control.

The Great Fire of London had several important results. It finally stopped the disease which had killed so many people in 1665. It destroyed 87 churches, but it also burnt down about 13,000 wooden houses, which were neither safe nor healthy. After the Great Fire, more houses were built of stone, so London became a cleaner, healthier city.

The Great Fire also badly damaged one of London's most important churches, the old Saint Paul's Cathedral, so King Charles asked Sir Christopher Wren to plan a new cathedral. In 1675, Sir Christopher finally began the 'new' Saint Paul's, which still stands in London today.

Saint Paul's Cathedral after the Great Fire

2.2   The *Titanic*

'Unsinkable!' 'It will never go down!' 'The safest ship in the world!' 'A palace on water!'

Those were some of the words used to describe the *Titanic* before she sailed on her first journey on 10 April 1912. She had more than 2,220 people on board when she left Southampton in England for New York in the USA.

The *Titanic* was indeed a special ship. Her rich first-class passengers enjoyed furniture and rooms that were like those in a palace. There were libraries, restaurants, sitting rooms, reading rooms, and a swimming pool on board. Like all big passenger ships, the *Titanic* had radio, which was used by Captain Edward Smith and the crew to keep in contact with the land. Later in the journey, of course, radio would help to save hundreds of lives when it was used to contact other ships.

Not all the *Titanic*'s passengers were rich. Many second-class and third-class passengers were hoping to start a new and better life in the USA. The poor third-class passengers had very small rooms deep down in the ship, and their living conditions were very basic.

On Sunday 14 April, after five days at sea, the *Titanic* was in the freezing north Atlantic, about 2,000 kilometres east of New York. It was springtime, and Captain Smith knew that ice sometimes appeared in the sea at this time of year. But he was confident that ice was not a real danger. After all, the *Titanic* was unsinkable!

As it was Sunday, the passengers and crew went to church

in the morning, then they returned to their normal routine. Men played cards, and ladies laughed and talked, while they enjoyed beautiful music. Rich passengers sent radio messages to their friends in New York and London. Captain Smith was invited to a dinner party.

During that cold evening, the *Titanic* received seven radio messages warning of the danger of ice. The captain heard at least one of the warnings, but he ordered the ship to continue straight towards New York.

Later that night, the look-out boy saw an iceberg – a great mountain of ice in the sea. He rang the alarm bell

Inside the *Titanic*, 1912

immediately and at last the captain and the crew took the
warning of ice seriously. The captain immediately tried to
turn the ship away from danger. Too late! The attempt was
hopeless. The *Titanic* was huge and heavy: 268 metres long,
32 metres high, and over 47,000 tonnes. There was simply not
enough time to turn the ship and avoid the iceberg.

A few minutes before midnight, the *Titanic* crashed into
the iceberg, and a hole 90 metres long appeared in the ship's
side. When the captain went to see the hole and saw water
entering the ship, he immediately ordered the crew to get
the lifeboats ready – although he knew that there were only
enough lifeboats to save just over half the people on board.
At 12.15 a.m. the first radio messages went out, asking for
help.

There was so much music and noise on board the *Titanic*
that the passengers did not at first notice that the engines
were strangely silent. It was half an hour before the first-class
passengers realized that anything had happened. The crew
went down the stairs to warn the poorer passengers, who
then desperately tried to find their way up to the lifeboats.
For some people, the long journey up through the ship took
more than an hour.

When the lifeboats were ready, women and children were
ordered to get in first. Many families were separated, and
many children never saw their fathers again.

Edith Brown, aged fifteen, was with her rich parents
Thomas and Elizabeth Brown, who had decided to start a
new life in the USA. Before the journey, her father had had a
bad dream about the idea, but her mother had decided that
they must go. Thomas Brown's face was white as he boarded
the *Titanic* at Southampton, and again he looked white when
he entered the family's room that cold night. He told Edith

One of the *Titanic*'s lifeboats, seen from the *Carpathia*

and Elizabeth to put on warm clothes, because the ship had hit an iceberg. The family left all their valuables on the ship. 'I'll see you in New York,' Thomas said, as Edith and her mother escaped to a lifeboat, but Edith never saw her father again.

From their lifeboat, Edith Brown saw one end of the ship sink into the freezing water. Suddenly all the lights went out, and where there had once been laughter and light, there were only screams and darkness.

As the sun rose the next morning, Edith, her mother, and the other survivors saw a sea full of bodies and icebergs. She and her mother were picked up by the *Carpathia*, the ship that received the *Titanic*'s radio calls for help. In the early hours of 15 April, the *Carpathia* saved 705 people from the cold Atlantic waters.

Edith Brown's experience of the *Titanic* disaster changed her life for ever. For a long time she had terrible dreams about that night in the Atlantic. Five years after the disaster she married Frederick Haisman, and together they had ten children. At the age of ninety-nine she travelled by ship with one of her daughters to the place where the *Titanic* sank, and she dropped a rose into the water as she remembered her father. She died in 1997, aged 100.

No survivors of the *Titanic* ever forgot their experience of the disaster. Five-year-old Lillian Asplund was travelling with her parents and her four brothers. They were in third class, where only twenty-three out of seventy-six children survived. When they reached the top of the ship, most of the lifeboats were full, so the family decided that they would die together. However, one of the crew separated them, and he threw Lillian and her smallest brother into a lifeboat. Lillian's father pushed his wife in with them, but then the lifeboat was lowered into the water. When Lillian's mother looked around, she only saw Lillian and her little brother. She never saw the rest of the family again.

Lillian, her little brother, and her mother stayed together for the rest of their lives. Her mother died on 15 April 1964, exactly fifty-two years after the *Titanic* sank in 1912. Neither Lillian nor her brother married.

Over 1,500 people died in the *Titanic* disaster. Many women and children survived, but many men died, both passengers and crew. Among the dead passengers were three extremely rich Americans – millionaires J. J. Astor, Isidor Straus, and Benjamin Guggenheim. Together, their fortunes were worth 600 million US dollars in 1912!

Captain Smith was among those who died. After the disaster, it was agreed that Captain Smith had been too confident, and not prepared for danger. A few years later, an international organization was started, so that ships would be better informed about icebergs. And after the *Titanic* disaster, all ships were ordered to carry enough lifeboats to save all the people on board.

The final resting place of the *Titanic*

The *Titanic* is still remembered today. There have been many books, films, and TV programmes about the story, and if you use your computer to search for the name *Titanic* you will find millions of results.

Many people searched for the resting place of the great ship, nearly four kilometres under the sea. The *Titanic* was finally found in 1985 by Dr Robert Ballard. Since then there has been much discussion and argument about what should be done with all the beautiful things that were on board. The families of survivors have been very angry that other people want to make money from all the things that were discovered with the ship at the bottom of the sea.

Yet nearly all the people who remember the ship, its journey, and its passengers have died, and so the arguments and discussions have quietened down. In January 2008 just one passenger who survived the sinking of the *Titanic* – Millvina Dean – was still alive and living in England. And as time passes, what remains of the great ship slowly falls apart, deep down on the ocean floor. The sinking of the *Titanic* will always be a powerful story, but when there are no more living survivors, it will be part of history.

2.3 Bhopal

Bhopal is a city of nearly 700,000 people in the middle of India. During the 1970s and 1980s, the American company Union Carbide had a large factory in Bhopal which made chemicals for industry and for farmers. Some of the chemicals that were made in Bhopal were insecticides, which kill insects, and some of them were extremely dangerous.

One of the chemicals, methyl isocyanate, was kept in special boxes under the ground. If the temperature was hotter than 38°C, the methyl isocyanate would become a deadly gas and it would escape into the air.

In December 1984, workers were busy repairing the special boxes for the methyl isocyanate. But at eleven o'clock on the night of 2 December, one man noticed that the temperature of the methyl isocyanate was rising above 38°C. He and several other workers tried to bring the temperature down, but it was too late. Just before one o'clock on the morning of 3 December, the deadly methyl isocyanate began to escape into the air.

Workers in the Union Carbide factory began to panic. Their eyes were burning, and it was difficult to breathe. The clouds of deadly gas began to move silently through the night air, passing over the poorer parts of the city. Hundreds of people died in their sleep. Homeless people who had been hoping to spend a warm night at the railway station continued to sleep, never to wake again. The station manager told a train driver not to stop at Bhopal. In this way he saved hundreds of lives before he himself died.

People living near the chemical factory thought that the end of the world had come. Thousands tried to escape from the city. In cars, in buses, by bicycle, or on foot, they moved as fast as they could away from the city of death. Their stomachs were sick, their eyes were blind, and they could not breathe. Many started the journey but never finished. Some escaped the city but then died a few hours later.

By seven o'clock that morning, 20,000 people had arrived at Hamidia hospital in Bhopal. But there were not enough medicines or doctors, and many people died while they were waiting. Survivors came to the front of the hospital where the bodies of the dead were placed, and searched for their loved ones.

Many other people never reached the hospital. Dead bodies of both animals and people lay all over the streets of the city.

A Bhopal victim

'I thought I had seen everything,' said a soldier in the Indian army, 'but this is worse than war.'

Who was to blame? A few days after the disaster, the American head of Union Carbide flew to Bhopal. He was immediately arrested, but he was allowed to go free after six hours. Many people in India still blame the American company for the disaster. However, the question is not so easy to answer.

The American company said that the safety system was the same for all their factories – in India, the USA, Brazil, or anywhere else in the world. The only difference was the way the safety system was managed. For many years the Indians continued to blame the American company and tried to get money from them. Then finally, in 1989, Union Carbide agreed to pay 470 million US dollars. This money is managed by the government of India for the Bhopal victims. But all the money in the world can never bring back the people who died in one of the worst industrial accidents in the world.

Between 5,000 and 15,000 people died in the Bhopal disaster, and at least 40,000 people suffered from serious illnesses as a result. But in addition to the problems that everyone can clearly see, thousands of people have suffered the most terrible dreams for many, many years after the disaster.

In 1984, Sunil Kumar Verma and his family were living opposite the Union Carbide factory. His parents, two of his brothers, and three of his sisters all died in their sleep during that awful night. He himself was rescued from a mountain of dead bodies which were ready to be burned. He managed to find his little sister and his baby brother, and he realized that at the age of thirteen, he was suddenly the head of his family.

Through many years of suffering, Sunil managed to work and to study. But he never forgot the tragedy that changed his family and his city. Although he did not have much money, he helped his brother and sister through school, and his door was always open to others in need.

Together with other survivors, Sunil and his friends made contact with many people who were willing to help the suffering people of Bhopal. He even made journeys to the USA

and Europe in order to tell the true story of the tragedy. Those journeys made the Bhopal disaster well known all over the world, and in that way, Sunil helped to make money to build the Sambhavna Trust Clinic. This special hospital offers medicines and other much-needed help for the survivors of the Bhopal disaster.

But behind his brave face, Sunil's heart continued to feel the cost of the tragedy that changed his life. For many years, he had been hearing voices in his head, and he believed that people were planning to murder him. Finally, on 17 July 2006, at the age of thirty-four, he took his own life. When his body was found, he was wearing his favourite T-shirt, which said 'No more Bhopals.'

There is no doubt that during his short life, Sunil Kumar Verma helped to make the world understand more about the dangers of chemical factories, and he brought great help to those who suffered. He did not die for nothing.

The Sambhavna Trust Clinic

2.4 *Challenger* and *Columbia*

During the 1950s, scientists from both Russia and the USA were working hard to find ways of sending people into space. The first man to go into space was Yuri Gagarin, a Russian astronaut who flew round the earth in 1961. Then in 1969 the American astronaut Neil Armstrong became the first person to walk on the Moon.

Since then, many astronauts have travelled in space, and many children and adults have imagined becoming an astronaut one day. For most people, this idea remains a dream. Normally, only very experienced scientists or very rich people travel into space. One example is Anousheh Ansari, a businesswoman from Iran, who paid more than 10 million US dollars for an eight-day journey into space in September 2006.

Challenger, 1986 In the 1980s, the USA began its space shuttle programme, which carried out many scientific experiments in space. The American government decided that the *Challenger* space shuttle would take not only scientists, but also a 'normal' person into space. This was a way of helping the American people to accept the great cost of the space shuttle programme.

In 1984, President Reagan of the USA decided that the 'normal' person should be a teacher. More than 11,000 teachers wanted the job, and the person who was finally chosen was Mrs Christa McAuliffe. While she was in space, she was going to give two 15-minute lessons by television, so that people all over the USA could understand the many advantages of space travel.

'I'm so excited!' she said. 'I don't think any teacher has ever been more ready to give two lessons than I am now. I've been preparing these since September and I just hope everybody watches this teacher teaching from space.'

The scientists on board *Challenger* had many important jobs to do, too. *Challenger* was going to help other space shuttles to keep in contact with Earth. There were experiments which studied different types of light, some which studied radiation, and others which measured how heavy chicken eggs are in space.

Challenger's crew: (back row) Ellison Onizuka, Christa McAuliffe, Greg Jarvis, Judy Resnick, (front row) Michael Smith, Dick Scobee, Ron McNair

Challenger had already been into space nine times before. This time it was going to take off in July 1985, from Florida, one of the warmest places in the USA. However, there were many delays until the final date was decided: 22 January 1986. Then new problems delayed the start again. Finally, on Monday 27 January 1986, the chief scientists decided that the shuttle was ready to go. Early that morning, the crew climbed into the space shuttle and waited for take-off.

The television cameras, the scientists, and the families of the astronauts were all in Florida, waiting to watch *Challenger* disappear into the sky. Christa McAuliffe's son Scott, aged nine, her daughter Caroline, aged six, her husband, her parents, and some of her students were all there.

But the scientists were worried about the door-locks, and they had noticed that the weather had brought clouds and high winds. So after five long hours on board, lying on their backs and waiting for take-off, the crew were asked to leave *Challenger*. Disappointment yet again.

The night of 27 January was a very difficult one. The *Challenger* crew were excited and tired, and the captain was really worried about the unusually cold weather. He had even seen ice on the space shuttle at night – something quite unexpected in Florida at that time of year.

The next morning, Tuesday 28 January 1986, the astronauts said goodbye to their excited families one more time. The scientists were still worried about the weather, but they decided to go ahead. At last, things started to happen. With forty-five seconds to go, the main engine started and the computers were in control. Then the countdown started. Ten . . . nine . . . eight . . . seven . . . six . . . five . . . four . . . three . . . two . . . one . . . and *Challenger* took off into space.

Everybody's first feelings were of perfect joy and excitement.

After one minute, the shuttle was flying higher and higher up into space. A little later, a small orange light was seen on the television screens, an unexpected light . . . Then it was not just a small light, but red and orange fire, followed by a cloud of white smoke. Suddenly the screens showed nothing, and all contact with *Challenger* was lost.

It was some time before anybody really accepted that a disaster had happened. Everybody wanted to believe that the shuttle and everyone inside would come back safely. But that was only a dream. The truth was hard to believe. *Challenger*

Challenger explodes

had exploded 73 seconds after take-off. Christa McAuliffe and the six other astronauts were dead.

Christa McAuliffe had caught the imagination of the whole nation, because she was just a normal American like anybody else. Jay Schaeffer, a teacher from Los Angeles, explained that for students everywhere, a teacher in space becomes *their* teacher: 'Do you know an astronaut? Everyone knows a teacher.' With the death of Christa McAuliffe, the American people lost confidence in the space programme.

In the days that followed, many nations of the world sent messages to President Reagan and to the families of the astronauts, expressing their sadness. 'When something like this happens,' said a Russian woman in Moscow, 'we are neither Russians nor Americans. We all just feel sorry for those who died and for their families.'

A few weeks later, the bodies of the astronauts were found with the many pieces of *Challenger* at the bottom of the Atlantic Ocean. The search cost 20 million dollars, but America could not rest until the bodies had been found.

The cause of the disaster was discovered quite quickly. At the time of the flight, the weather was freezing, and the cold had weakened the join between two parts of the shuttle. Oil escaped, and this caused the fire.

The *Challenger* was not only a disaster for the families of the seven astronauts. It was a disaster for the *Challenger* space programme, which had cost 1.2 billion US dollars to develop. In future, the space programme would find it more difficult to get money from the US government.

However, the disaster could not completely stop the USA's space programme. As President Reagan said on television, 'There will be more shuttle flights . . . more teachers in space. Nothing ends here. Our hopes and our journeys continue.'

***Columbia*, 2003**   After the *Challenger* disaster, the USA had more than eighty successful space flights. Several of these flights were made by *Columbia*, the oldest American space shuttle. Then in January 2003, *Columbia* took off on its twenty-eighth flight with seven astronauts on board.

Of course, the flight was not only about adventure and excitement but also about science. In fact, the crew on board *Columbia* took turns to sleep and work so that they could

Columbia waiting for take-off

successfully complete eighty valuable scientific experiments during their sixteen days in space. Some of the experiments collected information which was sent back to earth during the flight. Other experiments involved bringing materials back from space.

After their sixteen days in space, the astronauts on board *Columbia* were feeling very happy. Captain Rick Husband said, 'Things are going really great . . . We're having a great time up here. We had a great ride, and all the . . . experiments went extremely well . . .'

As the excited space travellers prepared to return to Earth, they were all looking forward to seeing their families again. But as the shuttle came closer to the Earth, the unthinkable happened.

At take-off, part of *Columbia's* wing had been damaged, but during the flight, this did not cause problems. When the space shuttle approached the Earth, however, hot gases came into the shuttle through the damaged wing, and it exploded in mid-air. Pieces of the shuttle were found in three states of the southern USA: Texas, Louisiana, and Arkansas.

After the horror and the sadness of the *Columbia* disaster had died down, President George W. Bush decided that seven small asteroids (pieces of rock that go round the sun) would be named after the seven astronauts who had died. In one sense, this means that the names of the brave astronauts will continue to live for ever.

The famous scientist Stephen Hawking (see page 1) believes that space discovery is not just for enjoyment: it is necessary for the human race to survive. He believes that human beings need to travel out into space and start new cities there. Perhaps that is why space adventures continue even after the *Challenger* and *Columbia* disasters.

2.5   The *Exxon Valdez*

When we think of Alaska, most of us think of a faraway land in the frozen north-west of America. A land of clear seas and skies, and great natural beauty.

This rich land makes its money from four things: fishing, forests, the tourist industry, and oil. On the south coast of Alaska is the port of Valdez, and from here most of Alaska's oil is taken by sea in big tankers to California and other parts of the USA.

On 24 March 1989, Captain Jeff Hazelwood was in command of an oil tanker which had the same name as the port of Valdez. The ship was owned by the Exxon oil company, so it was called the *Exxon Valdez*. Captain Hazelwood was an experienced seaman who had loved the sea and sailing since he was a child. When he was thirty-two, he became the youngest man to take command of an Exxon oil tanker.

Although Captain Hazelwood was an excellent seaman, he had a history of drinking too much alcohol. In fact, at the time of the *Exxon Valdez* disaster, Captain Hazelwood was not allowed to drive a car because the police had caught him drunk while driving. However Captain Hazelwood was still allowed to be in command of a tanker.

The sea off the coast of Alaska is always dangerous because it is full of small islands and rocks, some of which lie hidden under the water. In winter and spring, there is another danger: ice.

In the late evening of 24 March 1989, the *Exxon Valdez*

The *Exxon Valdez* in Prince William Sound

started on its normal journey from Alaska. At first, Captain Hazelwood was in control of the tanker, but later he went to do some paperwork, leaving the ship under the command of Third Officer Gregory Cousins.

Just after midnight, when the *Exxon Valdez* had entered Prince William Sound on the beautiful southern coast of Alaska, the tanker suddenly hit a group of rocks called Bligh Reef. The *Exxon Valdez* had five holes in its side, and one of them was 2 metres wide by 6 metres long. The captain sent a message: 'We're losing some oil, and we're going to be here for a while.' That was only a small part of the truth. In fact, 50 million litres of oil had begun to flow out of the tanker and into the sea.

Unfortunately, work to stop the oil spill did not begin immediately. A special boat that was kept in Valdez for emergencies had been damaged by a storm, and could not be used. So the clean-up began fifteen hours after Captain Hazelwood first reported the oil spill. The first two days after the spill, the sea had been calm and still; but by the time all the necessary machinery was in place, the weather had turned stormy. Strong winds quickly moved the oil to other parts of the sea, and the head of the Exxon oil company told the newspaper and television reporters that the company had a real problem on its hands.

The oil from the *Exxon Valdez* disaster found its way onto nearly 1,700 kilometres of Alaska's coast and it covered 4,800 square kilometres of water. It was the worst environmental disaster in American history; millions of fish, 300,000 sea birds, and thousands of sea animals died. Some animals and birds died of cold, because when the oil covered their bodies they could not keep warm. Others died of hunger, since 25 per cent of the plankton in the sea were destroyed in the disaster. (Plankton are very small plants and animals which live in the sea. They are an important part of the food chain: small fish eat the plankton, and are then eaten by bigger fish, which are eaten by people.)

However, the disaster did not only have an effect on animals, it also changed the lives of the people living in villages near Prince William Sound. Until the end of the nineteenth century, most of the people of Alaska had had no contact with the modern world. They have always lived by hunting and fishing, and their lives depend on the seasons and the sea. During the twentieth century, their lives changed when contact with Americans and Russians introduced new diseases into their lives – diseases which killed large numbers

Cleaning up after the oil spill

of people. Their lives changed again when there was an earthquake and tsunami in 1964. But their lives have changed even more because of the oil industry.

Chief Walter Meganack, the head of a village near Prince William Sound, explained how people in the villages in Alaska feel about their way of life: 'We are a part of nature. We don't need a calendar or clock to tell us what time it is . . . The birds returning from their winter holiday tell us, the daylight tells us. The roots of our lives grow deep into the water and land. That is who we are. The land and the water are our sources of life.'

All that changed because of the *Exxon Valdez* disaster. The people of Alaska describe the *Exxon Valdez* disaster as 'the day the water died'. Chief Meganack said this about the disaster: 'What we see now is death, death not of each other, but of a source of life, the water. We will need much help, much listening in order to live through the long . . . season of dead water, a longer winter than ever before. I am an elder. I am a chief. I will not lose hope. I will help my people. We have never lived through this kind of death, but we have lived through lots of other kinds of death. We will learn from the past, we will learn from each other, and we will live. The water is dead, but we are alive, and where there is life there is hope.'

It is easy to blame Captain Hazelwood for the *Exxon Valdez* disaster, and there is no question that he was responsible for the tanker at the time of the disaster. But it is also true that mistakes made by different people in the oil industry, both on land and at sea, played a part in the disaster. Many businessmen said, 'There has never been a disaster, so a disaster will never happen.' So people were not well prepared for the oil spill, and as a result there was a lot of unnecessary delay and damage.

In fact, there is an argument for saying that all of us have a part to play in disasters like the *Exxon Valdez*. We all use oil every day of our lives – in our homes, at work and play, and when we travel. It is our need for oil that causes beautiful places like Alaska to be opened up and developed.

Every nation needs energy for travel and industry, and to make electricity. That energy must come from somewhere – from the sun, wind, water, oil, gas, or nuclear energy. The need for cheap energy means that oil companies are always trying to keep costs down. This often means that people work longer hours, and perhaps they do not work as carefully as they should. Sometimes the result of this is a serious accident.

In fact, there have been other serious oil spills since 1989, but the *Exxon Valdez* remains in people's minds because it has become a sign of the world's hunger for oil, at any cost.

2.6 Chernobyl

In the spring time of 1986, the city of Pripyat was full of children and roses. New industry had come to that part of Ukraine, which is very near to Belarus and Russia. More than 50,000 people from thirty-three different countries lived there, most of them under the age of thirty. Many new homes had been built, there was lots of work, and most people felt happy and hopeful. The biggest industry was a nuclear power station at the nearby town of Chernobyl. This made electricity for millions of homes and thousands of industries. In fact, the government of the old USSR was extremely proud of the Chernobyl nuclear power station. (The USSR was the country which governed many parts of Eastern Europe and Asia until 1991.)

The Pripyat and the Dnieper rivers flow near Chernobyl, and boats regularly travelled the 100 kilometres south to Kiev, the capital city of Ukraine. All around Chernobyl were many villages where people grew flowers and vegetables. Even people who worked in factories or offices went home and looked after their gardens in the evenings.

In those days, Hanna Kozlova was a young mother with a son and a daughter. They had been watching the workers in Pripyat build a fantastic new funfair with a big wheel that they hoped to ride on. 'Wow! That's going to be really fun!' they all laughed. The new funfair was going to open on 1 May, which is a big day of celebration in many parts of the world.

On the evening of 25 April 1986, lots of children and their

families offered each other 'peace cakes'. They collected money for peace, and wrote letters to the government asking for peace in the world. That was a time of real hope and love.

That night, Hanna went to bed very late. As she was trying to get to sleep, she heard a loud noise. For a moment, she thought that it was an explosion and that a war had begun. 'I went out – it was a beautiful night, the moon was shining, and there was certainly no war!' she said.

Then someone knocked on the door and told Hanna and her husband that there was a big fire at the nuclear power station. The fire, several kilometres away, was an extraordinary sight, and they watched it for a while from the windows of their flat. Then they went back to sleep, and went to work as usual the next morning.

In fact, that day, 26 April 1986, was the last day of a normal life for Hanna and her family. The years that followed would bring sickness, worry, pain, and fear, for them and for thousands of others.

In the first months of 1986, some of the scientists at the Chernobyl power station had decided to try an experiment. The power station consisted of four reactors – huge buildings which can be seen from many kilometres away. When a nuclear power station is working normally, the reactors get extremely hot, so they have a special cooling system to cool them down.

Very late at night on Friday 25 April 1986, the scientists began their experiment in reactor number 4, and this caused the temperature to rise. Then suddenly it began to rise higher and higher, completely out of control, until at 1.23 a.m. there was a huge explosion. That was the noise that Hanna Kozlova heard soon after she went to bed.

Chernobyl after the explosion

When reactor number 4 exploded, sheets of flame shot into the sky. Broken walls, roofs, and ceilings hung in the air above the red-hot reactor. Then there were more explosions. And more. The building surrounding the reactor was blown hundreds of metres into the air. And from the hole where the building had stood, a beautiful, blue-white light shot upwards into the night sky – dangerous radiation from the heart of the nuclear power station.

Twenty people were working at reactor number 4 that night. Engineer Alexander Yuvchenko went to the door of the reactor with another worker. 'There was just a wall and a door left. We were looking into open space,' he says. He was the first man to really understand what had happened. Another of the workers, Valeri Khodemchuk, was the first person to die. His body has never been found.

Two minutes after the first explosion, the alarm sounded at a fire station in Chernobyl. From top to bottom of the telephone room, hundreds of red lights, one for every room in the nuclear power station, suddenly lit up.

In just one hour during that first night, the level of dangerous radiation rose to 30,000 roentgen: that is enough to kill a person in 48 seconds! A team of brave firemen tried to fight the fire with water, but their job was hopeless. They were taken to hospital and lived for two terrible weeks. One fireman's eyes changed from brown to blue, and another fireman suffered from awful burns to his heart. Their bodies were so radioactive that everyone was afraid to be near them. Nobody even wanted to bury the dead. There were 186 firemen fighting the fires at Chernobyl; many died there, and most survivors became ill later.

Because it was hard to get real information about the accident at Chernobyl, people began to tell many wild stories – about thousands of deaths, and cities living in fear. In fact, the world beyond Ukraine did not hear about the accident from the government of the USSR. They heard about it from Sweden, where a dangerous rise in radiation levels was reported at the Forsmark nuclear power station. Similar frightening reports came from Denmark and Norway. The scientists of western Europe finally realized that the radiation was coming from Ukraine.

For several long days, the government of the USSR remained silent. On May Day 1986, all of the top people in Ukraine's government went to a festival in Kiev, and they all behaved normally. The government said absolutely nothing at all about the explosion and fires at Chernobyl. Things appeared normal – but the reality was very different.

However, after 2 May 1986 the government of the USSR

agreed that the air, food, and water around Chernobyl were radioactive, and that it was dangerous for people to stay there. During the first days of May, people in Kiev wondered why there were no buses in their city. In fact, 1,200 buses from Kiev and other cities had been sent to Chernobyl to take people to safer places. After the accident, about 135,000 people were moved from around Chernobyl.

On 12 May, just as the fire was finally coming under control, President Mikhail Gorbachev told the people of the USSR about the disaster. That meant that the clean-up could really start. It was much too dangerous to touch dead bodies and machinery, so they were left exactly where they lay. Then a few months later, a huge, thick wall was built around reactor number 4. Inside it lies a helicopter that fell into the reactor the day after the explosion, together with its crew of four men and a fireman who fell from the roof.

Hanna Kozlova and her family enjoyed the 1986 May Day celebrations, but she did not feel well. Then her son Viktor became sick, and she took him to the doctor. She could not believe his words: Viktor was suffering from radiation sickness and there was nothing the Ukrainian doctors could do to help. Hanna screamed and screamed when she heard the news. She refused to believe that her child could be so ill.

But then, slowly, Hanna began to accept the truth, and she decided to find help. She wrote letters to hospitals all over the world, and she finally made contact with a group of people in France who were trying to help victims of the explosion. The group paid for Viktor to travel to a hospital in Paris, where he had an operation that saved his life. Now the family celebrate with Viktor twice a year – once for his birthday, and once for the day he had the operation!

The problems of Hanna's family were not unusual after

the Chernobyl accident: Viktor was one of thousands of children who became ill. Many suffered from illnesses that nobody understood. As one doctor said, 'We began to look for books about radioactivity to find out what to do . . . The books said nothing about what doctors should do if there was an accident at a nuclear power station. The books were just stupid. They seemed to be written for children.'

Many children born of parents who cleaned up after the Chernobyl accident have died very young. There is radioactivity in mothers' milk, the children suffer from cancer, they have useless arms and legs, or they have weak hearts. Most received no medical help because the doctors did not know what to do, or did not have the right medicines. Many parents refused to keep their children, because they did not know how to look after them. Even in other parts of Europe, women who were expecting a baby in 1986 were worried about the effects of radiation on their children.

The problem is that radiation has entered the food chain. In fact, the United Nations believes that levels of radiation will be high all over Europe for many, many years. And tens of thousands of square kilometres of farmland in Ukraine, Belarus, and Russia still cannot be used.

In the end, the government of the USSR reported that 299 people were taken to hospital after the Chernobyl disaster, and that by 5 June 1986, 24 people had died from radiation. But the local people, the local doctors, and nuclear scientists do not believe that these are the true figures. In fact, one of the many tragedies of the Chernobyl disaster is the fact that people had no information, or not enough information, about the disaster.

During the first winter after the disaster, the wild animals had a wonderful time: with no people around, they could eat

The ghost city of Pripyat

The Pripyat funfair

anything they could find. People had left their dogs in their homes, because they thought they would come back after a few days. But nobody returned, and so the dogs became wild and dangerous. On the streets of Pripyat, where children once played, there are only wild animals now.

In fact, Pripyat has become a ghost city. The funfair was never opened on 1 May, and there are no laughing children on the big wheel. The boats that used to travel to Kiev go nowhere now, and the clock above the city's swimming pool remains frozen at six minutes to twelve. There are no more roses. Grass grows up through the roads, and trees grow out of broken buildings. In one building, photos of people from the old USSR government lie on the floor where they fell that day. No hunting is allowed in the countryside around Chernobyl, and 500 square kilometres around it are guarded by government soldiers. Some people, however, have gone back to live in their old homes near to Chernobyl. Many of them are already ill, and they prefer to live their last years in a place that they know.

There is no doubt that the Chernobyl disaster was caused by human error. The power station was not safe, and the experiments that scientists were doing there were dangerous. To make matters worse, the workers at the power station did not know what to do in an emergency, and the government was extremely secretive.

Above all, the Chernobyl disaster was an environmental disaster. However, it also had a huge effect on the electricity industry everywhere in the world. There had been nuclear accidents before, and many people had said for years that nuclear power stations were dangerous. This was the first really big accident that proved their warnings were right. Soon after the accident, many crowds of people met together in European cities. They held up signs saying, 'Chernobyl is everywhere!' Suddenly governments had to think seriously about other ways of making electricity. That is why there is so much interest now in new types of energy.

The Chernobyl disaster was many years ago now, but its effects are still with us today in all kinds of ways.

3   Disease

For hundreds of years, people in Europe believed that disease was a punishment sent from God. However, in the twentieth and twenty-first centuries, Western medicine has come to understand that diseases spread because of contact between people, or between people and animals.

During the last two centuries, there have been many successful developments in science and medicine. Many of us will probably live longer than our grandparents did. However, as human beings, we cannot expect to 'play God'. People still fall ill, people grow old, and not many of us expect to live to the age of 100.

In this final part of the book, we consider disasters caused by diseases, and we take a special look at the modern tragedy of HIV/Aids.

3.1 Eyam and the plague

Birth, marriage, death; birth, marriage, death. That is the simple, basic story of human life. But in some times and places, people do not live long enough to marry, and death comes unexpectedly quickly.

In the north of England you can find beautiful countryside and many pretty villages. One of those villages is Eyam (pronounced Eem). Today the village has a school, a museum, several pubs, and many visitors. Some visitors come in summer to see the village well, where people used to get water

The village of Eyam today

from under the ground. This is because the villagers in Eyam have always made beautiful patterns of flowers and leaves around the well. But many people also visit Eyam for a very different reason.

During the years of 1665 and 1666, Eyam became famous because its people helped to prevent disease from spreading far and wide in the north of England. The disease, sometimes called 'the plague', had come to England from the Netherlands, and it killed one fifth of the population of London – over 65,000 people. Only the Great Fire of London (see chapter 2.1) stopped its spread in London. However, in 1666 one quarter of the population of England – about 2 million people – died from the plague. It was spread by a small insect called a flea, which lives on the blood of rats and humans.

During 1665, a parcel of cotton material from London arrived in Eyam for one of the villagers, a man called George Vicars. The material was wet, so Mr Vicars decided to put it in front of the fire in his home. As he touched the material, he felt a sudden pain – he had been bitten by a flea. Mr Vicars began to feel hot and cold, and red and black marks appeared on his skin. He went to bed, and in seven days he was dead.

But that is only the beginning of the story. More and more people in Eyam fell ill, and so the leader of the local church decided that the village should, if possible, have no contact with people outside the village. The sick were not allowed to go to the same meetings as the healthy. Families had to bury their own dead, in case the plague spread to others. People from outside Eyam brought food and left it near a well high above the village. When they had gone, the villagers collected the food and left money for it.

At least 260 people died of the plague in Eyam, and only

The Hancock Graves

86 survived. One of those survivors was Elizabeth Hancock, whose husband and six children all died in eight days. Elizabeth buried them all herself, and you can still visit their graves today, in a lonely field above the village. Because of the bravery of the people of Eyam, the plague did not spread to other villages in the north of England.

The plague that hit the village of Eyam had already come to Europe from Asia three centuries earlier. In the 1340s, the disease was so bad that it was called the Black Death. Over five years, it killed more than 25 million people – one quarter of Europe's population at that time.

In fact, this plague is just one of many in the history of the world. Many centuries ago, there were plagues in Egypt, which we can read about in the Bible and the Koran. There are also stories about how the armies of the powerful city-states of Rome and Athens lost thousands of men because of disease.

In modern Britain, young children still sing a song called *Ring a ring o' roses*. It is certainly an old song, and some people think that it comes from the time of the plague in London, or even the time of the Black Death, and that it is about dying from the plague. The children hold hands in a circle and sing:

Ring a ring o' roses,
a pocket full of posies;
atishoo, atishoo,
we all fall down!

The 'posies' in the song are handfuls of flowers, which people carried in their pockets to protect them from illness. The children pretend to be ill with a cold, so they sneeze ('atishoo!') and pretend to fall down dead. Then they get up and sing the song again!

3.2

HIV/Aids–
a modern plague

Thanks to modern medicine, good food, and better information about health, many people in places like Europe, North America, China, and Japan live until they are sixty, seventy, or even older. In the poorest countries of the world, however, many people only expect to live until their thirties or forties. In some parts of Africa, many parents see their children die before they do, because of our modern plague – HIV/Aids.

HIV/Aids is a disease of the blood. Many people get it from sexual contact, but you can also get the disease if blood containing HIV enters your body. When people first get HIV, they often seem to be normal and healthy. However, the body cannot protect itself against other diseases, and over a longer time HIV can develop into the deadly disease of Aids.

Aids is an even greater tragedy than the Black Death. In just one year – 2005 – it killed 3 million people, of whom a quarter were children. Two-thirds of the deaths were in the part of Africa that is south of the Sahara, and most were young adults. The disease is a slow killer, and in 2007 around 40 million people in the world were living with HIV. The numbers are rising every year. In a few years, it is expected that 25 million children will be left without parents – because of HIV/Aids.

But the great tragedy of HIV/Aids lies not only in the number of deaths, it also lies in the effects of the disease on the hearts and minds of people who suffer from it. People with HIV/Aids feel ashamed, so they do not speak about their problem. The result is they do not receive enough information from doctors and nurses. They are afraid to tell the truth, and so they silently pass the disease on to their families.

Many young adults have died, leaving their children to be brought up by grandparents. These young adults are the people who would normally earn money for their families and put food on the table. The result of so many deaths is that in many towns and villages in Africa and Asia nobody is earning money and keeping the village alive.

Sitsofe is fifteen. She and her brother Sellasie, who is ten, live in Ghana, West Africa. Their father died of Aids eight years ago and their mother died three years later. Their grandparents do not have enough money to care for their two grandchildren. Sitsofe says, 'I have lost all the happiness in my life: my dream is to become a nurse, but I don't think that is possible, because we have no money. And I don't want to get married because I'm afraid of getting HIV/Aids.'

Children without parents – the effect of Aids

Elizabeth is aged forty-two. She lives in Uganda, East Africa, and she has six children. For many years she earned money by selling vegetables at the market, but for the last twelve years she has been ill with HIV. This means that she feels weak, and her legs and arms hurt all the time. But she still tries to help her family: her cousin's wife died of Aids, so she looks after his young child as well. She would prefer to give rather than to receive help.

Elizabeth finds it difficult to choose between buying food and buying medicines, but she does not have enough money for both. Having the disease uses up time and money, and she cannot keep a job. So she is slowly sliding towards hunger and death.

Vitalis Ndusilo is twenty-nine and lives in Tanzania. He has HIV, but he feels very ashamed of the disease. He is too sick to work all the time, so there is often not enough money to live. He tries to get help from his church. 'Sometimes I walk down the street feeling very lonely. I just want to die,' he says. 'Then my friends tell me to remember that many of the people I pass in the street are in the same situation. But no one talks about it.'

Sometimes healthy people do not want contact with people who have HIV/Aids, because they are afraid of catching it. So for people with the disease, living with HIV/Aids can mean living with silence, loneliness, and misery. Silence stops people from helping one another with their problems, and it means that more and more people become victims of the disease. Until the silence is broken, people living with HIV/Aids will suffer even more.

In the 1980s, most of the people with HIV/Aids were poor and uneducated. People who had money and who were educated could try to protect themselves because they understood how to keep safe and they could afford to do so. However, the disease is slowly but surely reaching all kinds of people, rich and poor, educated and uneducated alike. It is passed from mothers to children, from husbands to wives, and from wives to husbands. The Black Death seemed to die out because people died more quickly than the disease could spread. But that does not seem to be true of Aids. It is a very 'successful' disease.

In many parts of the world, World HIV/Aids Day is celebrated on 1 December every year. On this special day, many people wear a red ribbon to show that they care for sons and daughters, brothers and sisters, parents and friends who have HIV/Aids. The actor John Barrowman says, 'I hope that by wearing a red ribbon, I will help to break down the wall of silence that surrounds HIV/Aids.' He believes that silence helps more people to catch the disease every minute. It is only by speaking out that we can stop the spread of HIV/Aids.

Disasters ahead

During the twentieth and twenty-first centuries, there have been many successful developments in science and medicine. We live longer. We have easy contact with people in different countries. We can travel quickly all over the world and beyond. Some of the scientific developments have offered new ways of preventing disasters – for example, warning systems for earthquakes and volcanoes. We also have new ways of helping people to manage the changes that result from disasters – for example, better medicines and better emergency foods.

As we consider these developments, let us return to the questions that Dr Stephen Hawking raised about the future of the human race.

After many people had considered his questions, Stephen Hawking also provided some of his own answers. There is the possibility of a nuclear disaster, for example, caused either by war or by the search for energy, and the possibility of spreading disease as a weapon of war.

However, Stephen Hawking also talked about another problem: the changes in our weather patterns on Earth, or climate change. Many scientists believe that our hunger for electricity and other kinds of energy is responsible for climate change, and this is causing more hurricanes and floods. Many people believe that climate change is a disaster that will change our patterns of spending, travelling, and living. Some even believe that climate change could destroy the human race.

We know that in the middle of disasters, people do help each other in extraordinary ways. Let us hope that, in reality, we shall be able to use the scientific developments of the twenty-first century to help each other, and to prevent the sorts of disasters that have been discussed in this book.

Climate change – a disaster ahead?

GLOSSARY

ash the grey powder that remains after a fire

astronaut someone whose job involves travelling and working in space

cancer a serious disease that often causes death

celebrate to show that a day or event is important by doing something special; **celebration** (*n*)

chemical a solid or liquid used in chemistry

class (here) a level of comfort for passengers in a plane, ship, etc.

crew all the people who work on a plane, ship, etc.

earth the world we live on; the substance plants grow in

earthquake a sudden violent shaking of the earth's surface

educated (*adj*) having had a high standard of education

energy a source of power, used for making heat, light, etc.

environment the natural world in which people, animals and plants live; **environmental** (*adj*)

erupt when a volcano erupts, it throws out burning rocks, smoke, ash, etc.; **eruption** (*n*)

experiment a scientific test that is done in order to study what happens

explosion the sudden violent bursting and noise when something explodes

festival a holiday when people celebrate a special event

flood a lot of water covering somewhere that is usually dry

funfair a kind of public entertainment where people pay to ride on big machines and play games for prizes

govern to have legal control of a country; **government** (*n*)

huge extremely large

human race all people on Earth, considered as a group

hunting chasing and killing animals and birds for food

industry the people and activities involved in producing goods or providing a service; **industrial** (*adj*)

mud wet earth that is soft and sticky

nuclear using or making nuclear energy

operation the process of cutting open a person's body in order to remove or repair a damaged part

panic to do silly or dangerous things because you are frightened

population all the people who live in a particular place

port a town or city with a harbour where ships can bring goods

power station a building where electricity is produced

powerful very strong

protect to make sure that somebody or something is not hurt or damaged

radiation powerful rays sent out from radioactive substances

radioactive sending out harmful radiation; **radioactivity** (*n*)

rat a small animal with a long tail, like a large mouse

reactor a large building used for producing nuclear energy

rescue to save somebody from danger

ribbon a narrow strip of material

science the study of natural things; **scientific** (*adj*) connected with science

sexual connected with a physical relationship between people

sink to go down under water

source a place where something begins or comes from

space the place beyond the earth where the planets and stars are; **space shuttle** a spacecraft designed to travel between earth and space several times

spread to affect more and more people, or cover a wider area

suffer to be badly affected by pain, sadness, disease, etc.

system a group of ideas or ways of doing something

tent a kind of small house made of cloth, used when camping

tragedy a very sad event or situation, often involving death

victim someone hurt or killed in a crime, accident, disaster, etc.

volcano a mountain with a large opening on top through which hot rocks, smoke, and ash are thrown into the air

well a deep hole in the ground from which people get water

Disaster!

ACTIVITIES

ACTIVITIES

Before Reading

1 Match the disasters with the definitions.

earthquake	When burning rocks, hot liquid and smoke come out of a volcano
eruption	A very large wave that goes over the land and destroys things
explosion	When oil accidentally goes out of a ship or a large container
flood	A sudden violent shaking of the earth's surface
oil spill	When something bursts suddenly with a very loud noise
plague	A disease that causes death and spreads quickly
tsunami	When a lot of water covers somewhere that is usually dry

2 Look back at the words in exercise 1. Answer the questions. Which of the disasters (if any) . . .

1 happened recently in your country?
2 happened a long time ago in your country?

3 Two of these sentences about disasters are correct. Which ones do you think they are?

1 The eruption of Vesuvius destroyed the city of Rome.
2 The Asian tsunami went as far as the east coast of Africa.
3 In 1995 there was an oil spill in the Japanese city of Kobe.
4 The explosion at the Chernobyl power station was in 2006.
5 After Hurricane Katrina there were floods in New Orleans.

ACTIVITIES

While Reading

Read Chapter 1.1, then rewrite these untrue sentences with the correct information.

1 Vesuvius is near the city of Milan.
2 The eruptions happened in August AD 379.
3 Pompeii was a poor town of 20,000 people.
4 Herculaneum was slowly covered by hot ash and rock.
5 Pliny the Younger wrote a letter about the disaster.
6 Pompeii and Herculaneum tell us a lot about Greek life 2,000 years ago.

Read Chapter 1.2, then circle a, b, or c.

1 A ____ man made the first machine to measure earthquakes.
　a) Japanese　　　　b) Chinese　　　c) Chilean
2 Before the Tangshan earthquake, ____ behaved strangely.
　a) babies　　　　　b) children　　　c) animals
3 The first earthquake in Tangshan lasted ____.
　a) 15 seconds　　　b) 50 seconds　　c) 15 minutes
4 ____ of the city of Tangshan was destroyed.
　a) A lot　　　　　b) Most　　　　　c) All
5 The Kobe earthquake started when many people were ____.
　a) in bed　　　　　b) at work　　　c) on holiday
6 After the earthquake a fifth of Kobe's population had no ____.
　a) water　　　　　b) food　　　　　c) homes
7 In Kobe ____ did as much damage as the actual earthquake.
　a) gas explosions　b) fire　　　　　c) water

Read Chapters 1.3 and 1.4, then fill in the gaps with these words.

August, days, December, earthquake, homes, hours, Hurricane, Indian Ocean, levees, lives, Mexico, Thailand, USA, waves

The Asian tsunami was caused by an _____ 30 kilometres under the _____ on the morning of 26 _____ 2004. There was a delay of several _____ before high _____ began to hit the coasts of Indonesia, _____, and many other countries. Hundreds of thousands of people lost their _____.

_____ Katrina started over the sea in the Gulf of _____ on 23 _____ 2005. It hit the coast of the _____ a few _____ later and damaged three of the _____ which protect the city of New Orleans. 80 per cent of the city became flooded and nearly 500,000 people lost their _____.

Read Chapter 2.1, then answer these questions.

1 When and where did the Great Fire of London start?
2 Why did the fire spread quickly?
3 Who wrote a description of the fire?
4 How did King Charles stop the fire?
5 Why was London a better place after the Great Fire?

Read Chapter 2.2, then circle the correct words.

1 The *Titanic* sailed from Southampton in *1902 / 1912*.
2 The ship received *seven / ten* radio messages about the ice.
3 On 14 April the *captain / look-out boy* saw a big iceberg.
4 The iceberg made a hole that was *nine / ninety* metres long.
5 There were enough lifeboats for *all / half* the passengers.
6 Many children never saw their *mothers / fathers* again.
7 Three famous *millionaires / film stars* died in the disaster.

Read Chapter 2.3, then match these halves of sentences.

1 In 1984, workers at the Union Carbide factory in Bhopal ...
2 On 3 December the deadly gas escaped and it ...
3 In the early hours of the morning, hundreds of people ...
4 By seven o'clock the next morning 20,000 people ...
5 When the head of Union Carbide flew to Bhopal, he ...
6 In 1989, the Union Carbide company ...
7 Sunil Kumar Verma ...

a died in their sleep.
b started to move silently through the sleeping city.
c agreed to pay the Indian government 470 million dollars.
d travelled around the world to tell the true story of the tragedy.
e began to repair boxes that contained methyl isocyanate gas.
f was immediately arrested but he was then allowed to go free.
g had arrived at the hospital in Bhopal.

Read Chapters 2.4 and 2.5. Choose the best question-word for these questions, and then answer them.

How many / How much / What / Who / Why

1 ... people were on board *Challenger* and *Columbia*?
2 ... was Christa McAuliffe going to do in space?
3 ... times had *Challenger* been into space before?
4 ... was the weather like before *Challenger* took off?
5 ... did the search for the bodies from *Challenger* cost?
6 ... did the crew of *Columbia* do in space?
7 ... did *Columbia* explode?
8 ... was in control of the *Exxon Valdez* when it hit rocks?
9 ... oil flowed out of the *Exxon Valdez*?
10 ... did the clean-up of the oil not begin immediately?
11 ... did the people of Alaska call the oil disaster?

Read Chapter 2.6. Put these events in the correct order.

1 The temperature of reactor number 4 began to rise quickly.
2 Gorbachev told the people of the USSR about the disaster.
3 A team of firemen came to fight the fire with water.
4 A huge, thick wall was built around reactor 4.
5 Scientists did an experiment at Chernobyl power station.
6 Many children born of parents who had helped to clean up after the disaster died young.
7 The world heard about the terrible accident from Sweden.
8 There were sudden explosions and a big fire.

Read Chapter 3.1 Are these sentences true (T) or false (F)? Rewrite the false ones with the correct information.

1 The plague came to England from the Netherlands.
2 The plague killed three-quarters of the population of London.
3 In 1665, George Vicars received a food parcel from London.
4 George Vicars was bitten by a flea and he later died.
5 People left food near the church high above the village.
6 Only 86 people survived the plague in Eyam.
7 The plague spread to other villages in the north of England.

Read Chapter 3.2. Then fill in the gaps with these words.

Africa, blood, contact, deadly, develop, food, healthy, sick, spread

HIV/Aids is a disease of the _____ which can be _____ by sexual _____. At first when people get HIV they often seem normal and _____, but over time they can go on to _____ the _____ disease of Aids. HIV/Aids is a very serious problem in parts of _____. Sufferers are often too _____ to work and find it difficult to get _____ for their families.

ACTIVITIES

After Reading

1 **Find these words in the word search below, and draw lines through them. They go from left to right and top to bottom.**

astronaut, cancer, chemical, crew, erupt, experiment, flight, iceberg, mud, nuclear, radiation, rats, reactor, sink, sneeze, tanker, tent

T	E	X	P	E	R	I	M	E	N	T
E	F	R	A	T	S	N	C	T	H	I
N	L	E	W	A	A	U	H	T	A	C
T	I	S	I	N	K	C	E	E	S	E
R	G	N	I	K	S	L	M	D	T	B
C	H	E	E	E	A	E	I	D	R	E
A	T	E	B	R	E	A	C	T	O	R
N	U	Z	T	W	R	R	A	E	N	G
C	A	E	R	E	U	A	L	L	A	M
E	C	R	E	W	P	I	V	E	U	U
R	A	D	I	A	T	I	O	N	T	D

Write down all the letters that do not have lines through them, beginning with the first line and going across each line to the end. There are 27 letters, making a sentence of 8 words.

1 What is the sentence, and who said it?
2 What had happened? Why did he say it?

Look again at the words in italics. Which stories are they from?

For example:
astronaut – the Challenger *and* Columbia *disasters*

2 The sentences below are about two young survivors of
disasters: Edith Brown and Tilly Smith. Put the sentences into
two groups and then put them in the correct order. Use the
linking words to join together pairs of sentences to make a
story about each girl.

and, because, but, so, so, when, when, where

1 Tilly was on the beach one day.

2 On 10 April 1912, Edith Brown and her parents, Thomas
and Elizabeth, left England on the *Titanic*.

3 Poor Thomas died in the water along with many other
people.

4 She had learned all about the signs of a tsunami at school.

5 Tilly returned to Thailand a year later.

6 They wanted to start a new life in the United States.

7 In December 2004, ten-year-old Tilly Smith and her family
went on holiday to Thailand.

8 Sadly there weren't enough places for everybody.

9 She spoke there to thousands of people about kindness and
bravery.

10 Edith and Elizabeth found seats in the lifeboat

11 She immediately warned her family and other tourists
about the danger.

12 The *Titanic* suddenly hit an iceberg on the night of 14
April.

13 They stayed in a hotel on the coast.

14 Edith never saw her father again.

15 She saw the sea was moving back very quickly from the
land.

16 Thomas immediately ran to his family and told them to
put on warm clothes.

3 Here are some newspaper headlines for some of the disasters
in the book. Which headlines go with which disasters?
Choose one of the headlines and write the first paragraph of
the article that goes with it.

SWEDISH SCIENTISTS QUESTION RADIATION
    MYSTERY
DEADLY GAS KILLS THOUSANDS IN SLEEP
HUGE EARTHQUAKE DESTROYS CITY
'UNSINKABLE' PALACE LOST WITH MANY MISSING
BRAVE TEACHER IN EXPLOSION TRAGEDY
SUPERDOME – WHO WILL HELP THE VICTIMS?
MODERN PLAGUE TOUCHES THE LIVES OF
    MILLIONS

4 Do you agree or disagree with these sentences? Why?

1 It is often poorer people who suffer most in disasters.
2 If people don't prepare for disasters, they cannot expect
help from the government.
3 There are always winners and losers in any disaster.
4 In the next hundred years there will be more frequent
disasters because of climate change.
5 In the future scientists will be able to prevent most disasters.

5 Find out more about a disaster that happened in your
country, or another disaster that interests you. Give a talk to
your class about it. Use these questions to help you:

– When and where did the disaster begin?
– What happened in the disaster?
– Why did the disaster happen?
– What lessons have been learned for the future?

ABOUT THE AUTHOR

Mary McIntosh loves adventures and languages. She especially enjoys the process of trying to understand how people from different cultures feel and think. In Nigeria, West Africa, she studied the Fulani language and then published a book about its grammar. On return to her native England, she worked for Oxford University Press creating books for teaching English, and was responsible for the very first books in the Oxford Bookworms Library when the series began. But it was not too long before she found herself travelling again, this time to Hong Kong. There she spent five years with her family and started writing books for language students in China and other countries in the Far East.

On her travels, Mary has been for a walk in a typhoon – which was exhilarating but highly dangerous. She has lived in a mud hut and experienced the harshness of life near the Sahara desert. Mary has two sons who also love travel. As well as writing books, she now works for a charity which helps people whose lives are affected by disasters in many parts of the world.

OXFORD BOOKWORMS LIBRARY

Classics • Crime & Mystery • Factfiles • Fantasy & Horror
Human Interest • Playscripts • Thriller & Adventure
True Stories • World Stories

The OXFORD BOOKWORMS LIBRARY provides enjoyable reading in English, with a wide range of classic and modern fiction, non-fiction, and plays. It includes original and adapted texts in seven carefully graded language stages, which take learners from beginner to advanced level. An overview is given on the next pages.

All Stage 1 titles are available as audio recordings, as well as over eighty other titles from Starter to Stage 6. All Starters and many titles at Stages 1 to 4 are specially recommended for younger learners. Every Bookworm is illustrated, and Starters and Factfiles have full-colour illustrations.

The OXFORD BOOKWORMS LIBRARY also offers extensive support. Each book contains an introduction to the story, notes about the author, a glossary, and activities. Additional resources include tests and worksheets, and answers for these and for the activities in the books. There is advice on running a class library, using audio recordings, and the many ways of using Oxford Bookworms in reading programmes. Resource materials are available on the website <www.oup.com/elt/gradedreaders>.

The *Oxford Bookworms Collection* is a series for advanced learners. It consists of volumes of short stories by well-known authors, both classic and modern. Texts are not abridged or adapted in any way, but carefully selected to be accessible to the advanced student.

You can find details and a full list of titles in the *Oxford Bookworms Library Catalogue* and *Oxford English Language Teaching Catalogues*, and on the website <www.oup.com/elt/gradedreaders>.

THE OXFORD BOOKWORMS LIBRARY
GRADING AND SAMPLE EXTRACTS

STARTER • 250 HEADWORDS

present simple – present continuous – imperative –
can/cannot, must – *going to* (future) – simple gerunds ...

Her phone is ringing – but where is it?

Sally gets out of bed and looks in her bag. No phone. She looks under the bed. No phone. Then she looks behind the door. There is her phone. Sally picks up her phone and answers it. *Sally's Phone*

STAGE 1 • 400 HEADWORDS

... past simple – coordination with *and*, *but*, *or* – subordination with *before*, *after*, *when*, *because*, *so* ...

I knew him in Persia. He was a famous builder and I worked with him there. For a time I was his friend, but not for long. When he came to Paris, I came after him – I wanted to watch him. He was a very clever, very dangerous man. *The Phantom of the Opera*

STAGE 2 • 700 HEADWORDS

... present perfect – *will* (future) – *(don't) have to, must not, could* – comparison of adjectives – simple *if* clauses – past continuous – tag questions – *ask/tell* + infinitive ...

While I was writing these words in my diary, I decided what to do. I must try to escape. I shall try to get down the wall outside. The window is high above the ground, but I have to try. I shall take some of the gold with me – if I escape, perhaps it will be helpful later. *Dracula*

STAGE 3 • 1000 HEADWORDS

... should, may – present perfect continuous – *used to* – past perfect –
causative – relative clauses – indirect statements ...

Of course, it was most important that no one should see
Colin, Mary, or Dickon entering the secret garden. So Colin
gave orders to the gardeners that they must all keep away
from that part of the garden in future. *The Secret Garden*

STAGE 4 • 1400 HEADWORDS

... past perfect continuous – passive (simple forms) –
would conditional clauses – indirect questions –
relatives with *where/when* – gerunds after prepositions/phrases ...

I was glad. Now Hyde could not show his face to the world
again. If he did, every honest man in London would be
proud to report him to the police. *Dr Jekyll and Mr Hyde*

STAGE 5 • 1800 HEADWORDS

... future continuous – future perfect –
passive (modals, continuous forms) –
would have conditional clauses – modals + perfect infinitive ...

If he had spoken Estella's name, I would have hit him. I was so
angry with him, and so depressed about my future, that I could
not eat the breakfast. Instead I went straight to the old house.
Great Expectations

STAGE 6 • 2500 HEADWORDS

... passive (infinitives, gerunds) – advanced modal meanings –
clauses of concession, condition

When I stepped up to the piano, I was confident. It was as if I
knew that the prodigy side of me really did exist. And when I
started to play, I was so caught up in how lovely I looked that
I didn't worry how I would sound. *The Joy Luck Club*

BOOKWORMS · FACTFILES · STAGE 4

Great Crimes

JOHN ESCOTT

It is more than forty years since the Great Train Robbery. Some of the robbers are dead, and only one – Ronnie Biggs – is still in prison. But there is still one thing that the police would like to know: what happened to the rest of the money that was taken? Two million pounds has never been found. Perhaps some of the robbers would like to know the answer to this question too . . .

Many great crimes end in a question. Who really killed President Kennedy? What happened to Shergar? Who knows the truth about Azaria Chamberlain? Not all the answers are known. Join the world's detectives and discover the love, death, hate, money and mystery held in the stories of the great crimes.

BOOKWORMS · FACTFILES · STAGE 4

Nelson Mandela

ROWENA AKINYEMI

In 1918 in the peaceful province of Transkei, South Africa, the Mandela family gave their new baby son the name Rolihlahla – 'troublemaker'. But the young boy's early years were happy ones, and he grew up to be a good student and an enthusiastic sportsman.

Who could imagine then what was waiting for Nelson Mandela – the tireless struggle for human rights, the long years in prison, the happiness and sadness of family life, and one day the title of President of South Africa? This is the story of an extraordinary man, recognized today as one of the world's great leaders, whose long walk to freedom brought new hope to a troubled nation.